S0-BUD-020

Mindful Kids

40 Fun and Beautiful activities to increase awareness, focus and calm oneself.

© Copyright 2018 - All rights reserved.

The content contained within this book may not be reproduced, duplicated or transmitted without direct written permission from the author or the publisher.

Under no circumstances will any blame or legal responsibility be held against the publisher, or author, for any damages, reparation, or monetary loss due to the information contained within this book. Either directly or indirectly.

Legal Notice:

This book is copyright protected. This book is only for personal use. You cannot amend, distribute, sell, use, quote or paraphrase any part, or the content within this book, without the consent of the author or publisher.

Disclaimer Notice:

Please note the information contained within this document is for educational and entertainment purposes only. All effort has been executed to present accurate, up to date, and reliable, complete information. No warranties of any kind are declared or implied. Readers acknowledge that the author is not engaging in the rendering of legal, financial, medical or professional advice. The content within this book was derived from various sources. Please consult a licensed professional before attempting any techniques outlined in this book.

By reading this document, the reader agrees that under no circumstances is the author responsible for any losses, direct or indirect, which are incurred as a result of the use of information contained within this document, including, but not limited to, — errors, omissions, or inaccuracies.

Table of Contents

Introduction to the Grown-Ups!

What is mindfulncss?

To be mindful is to be aware, to be *conscious*.

When we look at what this means and its implications we need to define being conscious and its context. Earth is a living, sentient entity and is a good reference as it shows that we are all *connected*. Life and all residing organisms are *one conscious entity*. This suggests that the whole purpose of meditation and mindfulness is to increase the qualities that make us connected.

Kindness, care, compassion, and empathy – these are all characteristics that define what it means to be *one with* the world and to be aware. It is essential when exploring different ways to be mindful, why you want to be mindful. 'Treat others how you wish to be treated' is the nature of this in its purest expression. If we are one conscious and connected entity, then surely one of our main aims in life is to develop and evolve ourselves to the best possible versions of ourselves, to our *highest possible frequency.*

And this is what this book aims to do. Children are already more in tune with the natural essence of the *Self* than some of us give them credit. The young frequently exhibit high levels of compassion and understanding far beyond the vibrational frequency many of us adults are operating at today. Many children see things we are not and are *in tune* with the more *invisible* and *extra*-sensory elements of thought, life, and awareness. It is us grownups who can learn a great deal from them.

This is a fundamental point to recognize before you start sharing mindfulness and meditation exercises with your children. Most of us are not raised with the practices, beliefs, philosophies, and everyday experiences that make one mindful and aware, *conscious* of our connection to the world in a spiritual way. It can arguably be suggested that we devolve, to an extent. In certain eastern cultures and religions, for example, Buddhist philosophies and interaction and observation of monks are an integral part of their daily life. Children grow up watching them. The monks, in their community, lead a more simple life with regular practice of kindness, compassion, and empathy as their mantra.

It is crucial therefore that we learn with them.

We are both the student and the teacher and practicing mindfulness and meditation with our kids (sometimes, they also need their space and to learn through self- autonomy and self- development) is very beneficial to them and in turn to us.

This book will explore practical and effective exercises for mindfulness. The activities can be used for a single kid, and groups of any size. The practices in these chapters are down to earth, highly accessible, and *uni*versal.

Your children will also be able to relate to the animals used to help them along their evolutionary journey. The path to self-mastery begins!

Introduction for the Kids

'Beauty is in the eye of the beholder.'

Don't you guys know it!

We, adults, tend to lose that unique quality kids have. We forget what it is like to 'be a kid,' to let go and have fun. I know the fact that I can still have fun playing with leaves, and climbing trees and so on. But not all of us do.

You 'kids' see the beauty in life and are more intuitive and intelligent than some of us grown-ups. So, I'm sure you are thinking, 'I know how to have fun.' I don't doubt this for one second! I also know how connected children are and how you see people, nature, and animals. We adults spend a lot of time and energy trying to get back to that state of mind. We secretly admire the child within you even though we don't tell you.

Now the more important question is: do you know how to be calm, and direct your awareness?

I know, it is easy to get distracted and let the

mind wander, especially with such an incredible imagination. But to 'be mindful' is to do pretty much what you do naturally, with an extra touch of magic!

So what exactly is mindfulness?

Mindfulness is being conscious, being *aware*. To be mindful is to recognize that all life is connected, and ultimately to wish to be treated with love, kindness, care, and compassion. Do you know how the sun makes you feel happy, warm, and full of life? And how the sea makes you feel calm or sparks your imagination?

This is because we are not separate from our natural world, but *connected* to it. We are *one with* it.

Being one with the world is a term you will slowly start to understand and integrate into your consciousness, into your *conscious mind*. Mindfulness can be used in many everyday situations from helping with homework and studies to the way you interact with your friends and peers. It can help bring greater focus, concentration, and understanding and also allow you to see the 'boring' or mundane tasks as fun. When we practice mindfulness, we become more *at peace* with the world, with people and our environment.

Allow the animal guides to help you on your journey! You may find it fascinating to know that many people in different cultures around the world see animals as our *spirit helpers*, unseen and invisible guides behind the scenes truly there for us to help with day to day problems, worries, and fears.

Your animal guides, *'Eli the Energy Elephant,' 'Freyja the Nature Fairy,' 'Solar the Fire Serpent,' 'Gracie the Garden Elf,'* and *'Melody the Water Whale'* will help you on your journey to mindfulness. Please don't be shy to call on them for help!

So here are the 40 fun and beautiful activities to increase awareness, focus, and calm oneself. *'Be mindful, be successful!'*

Fun fact!

Did you know that meditating effectively prior to an exam will help you achieve better results? *Truly*!

Your animal Guides:

Eli the Energy Elephant!

Freyja the Nature Fairy!

Solar the Fire Serpent!

Gracie the Garden Elf!

Melody the Water Whale!

Many people all over the world recognize the importance of animals and our connection to them. They see animals as having special superpowers, unique qualities we can connect with to assist us in daily life.

Call on your new animal friends to help bring more mindfulness and awareness into your activities. They are delighted to help.

Eli, the Energy Elephant, is your earth rock. He will help you with developing compassion, feelings of love and warmth, and increasing your connection to chi.

Freyja, the Nature Fairy brings magical feelings through the power of chi! She connects you to the trees, the animals and the forests in a way that is natural yet powerful. She is a gem!

Solar, the Fire Serpent aids in a fiery excitement of being alive. He helps chi flow through his connection to the sun, power, and vitality and can aid in creative and mindful expression.

Gracie, the Garden Elf, is your guardian! She brings comfort and a feeling of home. She reminds you of your connection to everyone and the natural world, lovingly and mindfully.

Melody, the Water Whale, helps heal and clear emotions. She will allow you to see things from a fresh perspective. In with the new! She also aids in imagination and creative expression, specifically with sound.

Chapter One: Breathing & Breath-work

Exercise: Breathe like a Dolphin

Imagine you are a dolphin. Why should you think of a dolphin?

It's because dolphins are beautiful creatures! Dolphins represent joy, playfulness, and a friendly community. They are always happy and possess high levels of compassion. They are also *intelligent and telepathic.*

Telepathy (*to be telepathic*) is the ability to communicate without words. Dolphins have supersonic radar which means they can communicate to their kin through the waves. Just as their speech travels through the ocean's waves, so do our thoughts travel through our mind. When we think we are also actively affecting, creating and shaping our physical world (fact!).

So if we are powerful creators and our thoughts affect the world in which we live, how does this relate to breathing and meditation?

Thought and breath are intrinsically connected. When we breathe we allow more air to fill up inside us. Air is also known as *energy* or *chi*. Chi is responsible for all aspects related to our thoughts, feelings, and beliefs.

Do you know why martial arts is considered cool? People who undertake martial arts can do some pretty incredible things that many of us believe cannot be accomplished by our body! The reason is that they work with chi, the *universal* and invisible life force.

So through *conscious breathing* and working on our breath, we allow ourselves to absorb more chi. This, in turn, makes us feel *lighter* and fuller with *force* and this further affects our mind.

We will look at many ways to help with mindfulness and all its benefits but, for now, imagine you are a dolphin. Imagine what it is like to be completely free, happy, and playful swimming through the sea. Picture what it feels like to be able to communicate through the waves. *Feel it*. Become the dolphin.

Now, sync your breath to that of the dolphins, still picturing the dolphin clearly in your mind and as if you are the dolphin. You should start to feel yourself fill up with more energy and feel much *lighter*. You could even feel floaty and euphoric or have sparked some incredibly imaginative ideas!

This exercise can be used if you need to develop a higher concentration in school, for focus in your studies or calmness before an exam. It can also be used for creativity, to aid inspiration and ingenious ideas, and to help with friendships and relationships amongst peers and family.

Try it for yourself!

Animal Guide: 'Melody the Water Whale!'

Exercise: Meditate for Magic

In later pages, we will go through real activities for mindfulness and meditation, but first, let's look at what it is.

What is mindfulness?

As briefly shared in the intro, to 'be mindful' is to be conscious. Earth itself is *one conscious living entity*, all living things on earth are connected through unseen and invisible forces. Just because you don't see something doesn't mean it is not real!

It is in the natural world where we best learn what being mindful is as our mind is linked to our feelings. When we *feel* our best, happy, joyous, at peace, generous, warm and connected to our friends and family, our minds are in a healthy and happy state. Our thoughts are influenced by our feelings just as our feelings are affected by our thoughts.

So in essence mindfulness is really about *harmonizing* the mind with the body and improving all aspects of life. There is an excellent truth in 'mind over matter.' Mind creates and affects matter!

Read one for some fun and mind-boggling exercises.

Exercise: Play with your Chi!

Play with your chi! Now, this one is enjoyable and can even be perceived as *magic*. As shared earlier, chi is used and cultivated by martial artists and is the source of *creativity and inspiration*. It can be seen as a '*superpower*' in itself as it is a genuine but unseen and invisible force.

To play with, and increase your chi, sit down in a meditative position. This can be either at home by yourself in your room, in a beautiful spot outside, or at school with friends (and of course in a group activity in class!). First, close your eyes and bring your hands up to your heart with your palms facing outwards. Start breathing, become conscious of your breath and allow it flow and be effortless. Once you feel relaxed and comfortable bring your attention to the palms of your hands.

As you are now relaxed and in a rhythmic flow with your breath you can multi-task. Rub your hands together, but not too vigorously. Do you feel the energy and heat in the palm of your hands?

If your answer was yes then, good. Now gently move your hands slightly away from each other and focus on your breath. Actively breathe into your palms, ***feeling and envisioning a ball of golden chi circling in between your palms***. Watch it expand.

This exercise can last anywhere from five minutes to fifteen. Keep the focus on your breath and the ball of golden chi perpetually expanding between your hands. The more powerful it becomes, the further away you can pull your hands. It should reach the stage where your palms are naturally pushed away from each other, like a magnet.

This is the power of chi!

To combine mindfulness with this exercise, choose a keyword to focus on. The beautiful thing about this activity is that it can last for such a long time and you can play with many different qualities.

Suggested qualities/words to increase and expand in your chi ball:

Imagination	Beauty
Kindness	Creativity
Compassion	Success
Empathy	Intelligence
Understanding	Achievement
Awareness	Patience

Whichever association you choose, *visualize* it in your ball of chi and use your *intentions*, the power of your mind, to watch it grow. Stay focused and connected to this ball of glowing light and the characteristics you are embodying and, finally, slowly bring it up over your head. Pour it over your head, allowing it to fill you up entirely and actively feel yourself becoming filled with this powerful, loving and glowing chi ball.

Epic.

Exercise: Tree Meditation

This profound yet straightforward exercise is perfect to practice breathing and increase mindfulness. It is also great for imagination and creativity!

Find your happy place. This can be in your garden or your favorite field, park etc. (make sure you are with your parents!) Find a tree that catches your eye. Now, sit on the ground with your back straight against the trunk and your knees bent with your feet on the ground (lotus posture). Remember your *posture.*

For more significant effect, go barefoot. Truly. The *invisible but powerful chi* flows through not only your spine and palms but also through your feet, directly into the earth. Get comfortable and start your breathing as practiced before.

Now, visualize yourself as this great, wise tree. Picture the top of your head as the sun and your feet as the earth. With each breath, imagine and envision air flowing up this tree's trunk from its roots to its leaves. With each out breath imagine the air flowing back down from the leaves to the roots.

This cyclic breathing may sound simple, but it may take some effort to get the hang!

The key is to be patient with yourself and take your time. The main goal of this exercise is to get to the stage where you are breathing like the tree is as natural as breathing without any conscious thought. Just as in 'Breathe like a Dolphin,' really *merge and synchronize* your breath with the visuals.

The effects of this tree meditation are vast, helping you with a wide range of life's problems. Positive benefits include greater focus and concentration on tricky or testing tasks, inner peace, and calmness of mind, calming emotions, and expanding awareness, increasing imagination, helping with creativity, increase in performance in learning and studies, and a more positive outlook towards life, people, and situations. It can also bring greater feelings of warmth and love!

Animal Guide: 'Freyja the Nature Fairy!'

Fun Fact!

Did you know science has shown us that trees, plants, flowers, and nature respond to human thoughts? We actively change nature's biological structure with our minds!

Chapter Two: Body Language

Exercise: Sit in Silence

Sitting in silence can be deeply therapeutic. Without silence, there would be no sound and without sound no silence. All thought, therefore, comes from silence.

This meditation exercise can greatly help with many, many aspects to daily life. Anger, irritability, unhappiness, a tendency to be aggressive; boredom, a lack of imagination, lack of concentration or focus, limited thinking in class, a lack of inspiration. Silence as meditation is a solution for all of these!

Combining mantras for mindfulness or positive affirmations works well with this. This is because when you are in silence you are a clear canvas, so you can 'fill up' your mind and emotions with the 'stories' you wish to tell yourself.

Life is a story; we tell ourselves stories every

day.

What sort of stories would you like?

Hint: ones full of love, happiness, connection, warmth, inspiration, and achievement!

Take some time to be silent and contemplate life's deeper meanings. See what magic arises.

Fun fact!

Some people travel across the world to go on silent retreats. They eat, sleep, socialize, meditate and clean for weeks without saying a single word!

Exercise: Watch the Clouds

There is a great deal that can be learned about ourselves through cloud watching.

When we watch the clouds, we are engaged in a form of meditation. As all the natural world is a part of us, a reflection of us, cloud watching allows the mind to wander and travel to infinite realms of our imagination. It is where *creative genius* can arise and, perhaps paradoxically, great *concentration and focus* can be gained.

This is because we receive a *sense of space* when we watch the clouds. Our minds fill up with emptiness and space for *creation*. This isn't a 'dark' emptiness, a feeling of gloom or unhappiness, but more a serene and *reflective emptiness*. This in itself increases *awareness* of ourselves and the world around us.

A fun activity to try when you next want to do some cloud gazing is to imagine you yourself are a cloud. This can be incredibly stimulating!

First, imagine you are one cloud. Keep your awareness on this one cloud. Then watch how it interacts with the clouds, and sky, around it. Next, imagine yourself as the surrounding clouds: all the clouds in your vision. Keep your focus on the first cloud but *merge* it with the collection of clouds in that area.

Sit with this for a while.

Finally, imagine yourself as the sky. Once you are the sky, shift your eyes to both the first cloud and all the clouds. Alternate between the two.

How do you feel? What thoughts and

impressions come up?

This exercise is *really powerful* for getting insight into your own mind, thoughts, feelings, and beliefs. It helps you see yourself as both the individual and collective, you yourself on your own journey and how you relate to and interact with the world, and you as part of and *one with* the world and your community.

If you really want to develop your awareness, write a poem about how you feel. You could call it 'Cloud Vision?' ☺

Animal Guides: 'Freyja the Nature Fairy!' 'Eli the Energy Elephant!'

Exercise: Remember your Posture!

As explored in chapter one, breath is extremely important when it comes to mindfulness. So how can we breathe properly when we have terrible posture?

Remember to sit up straight and *keep your back in a healthy position*. This simple activity really helps and in so many areas of life. It can greatly affect your studies, your ability to concentrate, creative and imaginative expression, and general performance in all aspects of school and learning. It also greatly improves your health and is preventative self-care for any future health problems in life.

It is through our spines that our *kundalini energy* flows. Kundalini is *the power serpent*, the *source of chi* and all of our energy. Without a free flow of this energy, we would not be able to function as the wonderful begins that we are. Chi energy needs to flow easily and effortlessly and by allowing it to do so you will notice how sharper, on point, and also imaginative your mind is.

Remember this *mantra* to include in daily life: '***Sit up Straight for Serpent Power***!'

Animal Guide: 'Solar the Fire Serpent!'

Exercise: Be Kind

The way we feel and think about someone

influences them greatly. Just through our attitudes and hidden opinions alone we actively have an effect on people, animals, and environments.

When we think something 'negative' or nasty about someone, they *subconsciously* react. It is like when you fling an elastic band- you don't physically see the air move but you know that the air is moving. This is the same for our thoughts!

Did you know that not only our thoughts but our beliefs actively radiate out to influence time and space? Science has shown us nowadays that our *energy*, our inner workings greatly affect the world around us. So when we are kind to others we are being powerful creators!

Being mindful of our attitude and energy towards others is a form of meditation in itself. Do you know how you feel when you have had a bad day and have acted particularly mean or hurtful towards someone? You don't feel good inside, do you? This is because that person is you!

We are all a reflection of each other, all *connected* on an invisible level. Practicing kindness, caring, and compassion is a beautiful meditation to integrate into daily life.

Fun fact!

Did you know that elephants mourn their dead? When a loved one dies, they stand in a circle and actively cry with sadness. They show extreme *compassion!*

Chapter Three: Observing Thoughts

Exercise: Imagine you are an Owl

Owls are magical birds. They can turn their heads up to 270 degrees and have a special night vision, so of course, we are going to connect to their energy and unique characteristics for our meditation!

To *be mindful* is to be in control of and connected to our thoughts. The difference between mindfulness and thinking is that, although they both involve thought, in mindfulness our thoughts are conscious. We are *aware* of them.

What better way to connect to our own thoughts than by embodying ourselves as the magical and mysterious owl?

As the owl is an animal of the night this exercise is best performed at night time, in the evening, or in darkness (turn the lights out).

First, familiarize yourself with the owl, either through a picture or by connecting deeper and drawing one. Once you are still inside and in a peaceful area, recite this poem.

'I see beyond what you do,

My vision is unique,

All things in your immediate sight

are replaced with mystery.

I see beyond the surface,

I know the things you hide,

Ask me to spell my secrets

Let moons magic be your guide.'

Now, once you are connected to the special *superpowers* of the owl, be still. Don't think anything. Just simply be in that state of stillness and inner calm. Then think this one thought: 'please, teach me something. I wish to learn.'

Your *intention* should be for knowledge, wisdom and truth, something unique and *unseen* that you may not have been originally thinking about.

From this deep space of silence, combined with the owl's magic, your *awareness* will now go to some topic, issue, belief, or thought that some aspect of yourself wishes to think about. These are the unseen and hidden things that wish to *come to light* (come to your conscious awareness).

Remember to say thank you to the owl!

Fun Fact!

Owls symbolize clairvoyance, mysticism, and magic! They are said to be *messengers of secrets* from the unseen worlds...

Exercise: 'If I was a...'

This is a great exercise if you wish to know more about yourself. You can explore different aspects of your personality, beliefs, and perceptions and how much you have learned integrated from your studies by connecting to different animals, people, and archetypes.

For example,

'If I was a horse.'

'If I was a musician'

'If I was a space explorer.'

You can then add whatever naturally comes to mind, such as 'if I was a horse I would enjoy being free.' If I was a musician I would love to travel the world.' 'If I was a space traveler I would enjoy exploring our planets and stars.'

Your answer, which will be unique to you, will provide you direct insight into your hopes, your goals, your dreams, and your inner wishes. They may also provide insight into your fears, concerns, and anxieties depending on your answers.

Take some time for this mindful meditation activity and create your list of 'if I was a...' Feel free to share it with your friends.

Animal Guide: 'Gracie the Garden Elf!'

Exercise: Become the Moon

As we briefly explored in 'Imagine you are an Owl,' the moon is a magical entity. All things hidden, unseen, and invisible relating to our *subconscious* link to the moon, therefore she is magic as there is a supernatural element to her, an element we cannot see with our physical eyes. (Note: Supernatural is just *natural* with a super!)

There are more than five senses and through meditation and observing our thought exercises we can really connect to the deeper places of ourselves. This specific mindfulness exercise, therefore, is for *awareness and understanding* of oneself.

'Become the moon' in whichever way feels best for you, either through art, poetry, or dance. With this one, you can really let loose and explore your artistic and creative side. Don't let anyone or anything stop you. This one requires complete freedom and expression (without harming anything, of course!)

Whichever outlet you choose; a drawing, a painting, a poem or an expressive dance, start with the breathing exercise from the first chapter. Once you are in your happy place (that calm space with easy breathing) imagine the moon.

How does she make you feel?

What emotions does she bring up?

Who or what are you thinking about?

Allow yourself to feel anything that wishes to arise. If it is positive, then beautiful. If it is something sad or negative, then don't worry, just use this as a learning process. Do try to focus on the warm, happy, and positive expressions of the moon for the best effect.

The purpose of this exercise is to connect to your *right brain*, the intuitive, instinctual, artistic, and imaginative aspect of your mind. We have both a logical and rational mind and an artistic, intuitive and 'dreamy' one. *When we connect to our right brain, we allow our awareness to expand and greater mindfulness is achieved*, which in turn allows us to perform left brain tasks with greater focus. Analytical tasks, problem-solving, and topics that call for logic and reasoning all come under the left brain. Most of the subjects taught in school! So connecting with your right brain by becoming the moon will help greatly and give your mind the balance it requires.

Animal Guide: 'Freyja the Nature Fairy!'

Exercise: Spirit Science

All life can be measured in terms of both *spirits* and of *science*. Spirit is the unseen and invisible force that construct physical life as we know it. Science is the concrete measurement of phenomena in our natural world.

The *spirit science* of mindfulness and meditation, scientific findings into the power of meditation and its positive effects are supported by many fascinating studies.

Exercise: Research the 'scientific studies and findings of mindfulness and meditation.' Prepare to be amazed!

Chapter Four: Language

Exercise: Start a Dream Diary

In dreams, we get to explore the inner workings of our *conscious mind*. We see directly into our *subconscious*, learn messages, and go on adventures! Symbols often present themselves to us in dreams and, if we are lucky, we will get shown our fears, and how to rectify them in daily life.

Dreams act as portals and can provide greater awareness, clarity, and solutions to life's problems. Through starting a dream diary, a journal of your dreams and any symbols or messages contained, you will begin a new journey of long-term mindfulness. Your dreams will act as reference points and you can return to them again and again for learning and self-development.

Of course, it's really fun to be able to re-live your best dreams!

Start a dream diary and integrate your animal helpers for assistance. They will help provide insight into the world of dreams.

Animal Guides: All of them!

Fun Fact!

Dreams can act as doorways to unseen worlds, connect you to loved ones, and provide you with direct messages and knowledge in daily life. *People also have pre-cognitive dreams. They see the future!*

Exercise: Mind Read!

Just like dolphins can speak telepathically through their thoughts, some *ancient scriptures* say that humans can do that too. That's an incredible thought, right?

Practice communicating through thought alone by 'sending' a specific word to a friend. This can be done in pairs when you are both aware.

Make sure your breath is steady, the mind is clear, and you have an inner calm before attempting this exercise. Set your *intention* and *focus*. First, try with something simple and easily received such as a color or shape. If you happen to be telepathic then you can evolve into more complex words and phrases!

Hint: _snakes sense sound waves through their tongues_! They are so connected to the natural world that they recognize there is more than physicality. They live in a world of _vibrations_.

Animal Guides: 'Eli the Energy Elephant,' 'Solar the Fire Serpent,' and 'Melody the Water Whale.'

Exercise: Be Neurological!

Meditation changes neurological activity in our brains. Let's reword that for effect: _meditation changes the structure of neurons in our brains!_

Neurons are responsible for our thoughts, feelings, emotions, and our beliefs. Essentially _everything is connected_, we are all one interconnected functioning being. You know if you eat too much food and you feel heavy, you then feel tired? Or when you are happy you feel more loved and connected to your friends and family? This is due to your neurons!

Whatever we do to our physical body affects our mind and our emotions. However, when we feel emotional it affects the thoughts we have and how we feel. The thoughts that we have affect our emotions and our physical wellbeing and energy levels. All of us are *connected*, an interweaving network of neurons, messages, and signals.

So it all comes down to that magical little word that you know holds so much power: ***chi***. When you meditate, you fill yourself up with chi, with energy and oxygen. This circulates around your cells directly affecting your thoughts, your feelings, and your emotions. This, of course, affects your life on every level!

Draw a mind map of the web itself as your brain. Write how you think each link is connected and what they stand for. Put it on your wall or somewhere you can access daily for learning and to help you with your relationships, unique gifts, and studies. ***Be neurological!***

Animal Guide: 'Eli the Energy Elephant!'

Exercise: Write your 'Self'

Write yourself, literally! The famous Carl Jung was one of the founding fathers of modern psychology (the way we think, respond to and interact with the world). He came up with a set of *universal archetypes*. These *archetypes* are characters and personas of *the Self*, the collective 'blueprint' which relates to every person here on earth.

So, what better way to explore the mind in a fun and stimulating way than to get creative with your own self?!

This exercise is pretty simple, yet effective. It can be done by yourself, with friends, or with peers at school in a group. The key is to remember that writing is in itself a form of meditation as *to meditate* is to *contemplate*.

Following Jung's list of archetypes, write what each of them mean to you. Be as open and honest as possible.

<u>Hint:</u> This one calls for mindful research!

Fun Fact!

Some people can consciously explore their dreams! They have trained their minds to the point that they are completely awake and aware in dream time.

Chapter Five: Shapes & Color

Exercise: Cook with Colors

Cooking can be such a mindful and creative process! Without going into detail about food, let's explore the *colors* and how each one can be connected to for certain *energy* (characteristics) to help in daily life. Refer to the color guide in the exercise 'Draw the Rainbow!' later in this chapter.

The One Month Challenge!

For the next 30 days become the chef of your house. Ask your parents to take you shopping and allow you to pick the foods (they can help though). Pick *only* foods that represent the rainbow, and preferably healthy foods like vegetables (this won't work with multi-colored sweets!).

Once a week, have a 'Creative Cooking' night with your parent or guardian. For this to work the criteria is: ***you must make a meal out*** *of the rainbow*! Think lots of vegetables, salads, nutritious and tasty foods like beans, lentils, chickpeas, and nuts and seeds if you like them. Buy *herbs* or *fresh living herb pots* and explore your senses and the different tastes of the world of herbs.

Get *creative* with cooking and develop a connection to those foods which are full of *life force*. Every week after your creative cooking night, take some time to contemplate and meditate on how you feel, how 'eating the rainbow' made you feel and your sensory responses to the different herbs and tasty healthy foods. Feel free to express your experience through art, drawing, or poetry!

Animal Guides: 'Eli the Energy Elephant,' 'Gracie the Garden Elf!'

Exercise: Make Art

Making art is one of the best ways to bring *greater focus*, *calmness,* and *awareness* as your mind is allowed to wander.

Through artistic and creative activities our mind enters a state of ease and *unlimited expression*. We are allowed to travel and explore different places and use the vastness of our imagination. This, of course, brings great calmness (in addition to some excitement) whilst also being an activity for focus.

Art is one of the few activities that really combines focus, paying attention to detail, and having a set goal with freedom and unbounded creative expression.

And there are so many artistic activities to choose from! Drawing, painting, writing, making, collaging, shading, experimenting with colors, objects and shapes...these all come under art's domain.

Choose what feels right for you and allows your *awareness* to wander. Explore all the various shapes, colors and patterns, and note what feelings, thoughts, and associations come up. Work with your animal guides, either subconsciously (not physically drawing them or connecting with them on a mental level) or physically draw or express them. You can also ask for their assistance and create their own qualities and 'superpowers' through your art.

Animal Guides:

Eli the Energy Elephant!

Freyja the Nature Fairy!

Solar the Fire Serpent!

Gracie the Garden Elf!

Melody the Water Whale!

Exercise: Visualize a Triangle

Shapes, or more specifically the triangle, can be meditated on to enhance awareness. *Visualization, imagination, and stillness of mind* are keys here. It's also really fun to do!

The triangle is very special in the world of spirituality, mindfulness, and developing self-awareness. This is because it is the triangle which is the building block of *consciousness*. It is the holy trinity, the three. It is also the fundamental shape from which all crystals and rare gems are built.

Meditating on a triangle does incredible things to the mind! *It increases focus, develops awareness, and can increase extra-sensory abilities* (think of the snake!). It can help expand the imagination and help remember dreams. *Focus, concentration, and the ability to hold onto knowledge* can all be increased by connecting to the triangle shape. It aids in learning.

To go to the next level in your awesome mindfulness abilities, merge the colors and their meanings into your envisioning activities. Don't forget to share the magic with your friends.

Animal Guide: 'Melody the Water Whale!'

Exercise: Draw the Rainbow!

Many ancient cultures, people dating back thousands of years, were aware of how certain things could be used for healing. This extends far beyond Calpol and medicines the doctors supply!

These people knew of the power of *color*, and more specifically how we ourselves embodied certain colors (just like a rainbow!). The ancients believed that our bodies are constructed of portals of energy, unseen invisible currents just like the tides and waves of the sea and cycles of the moon and stars. Each color contains specific energy, a *frequency* (think of the electromagnetic spectrum) and these subsequently relate to our own inner workings. Each color can be meditated on and connected to receive the qualities of the color. It may sound complex, but really it's pretty simple.

When you are outside in your favorite park or field you feel happy, don't you? There is a feeling of calmness and contentment/sheer joy and bliss. When at the ocean or seaside the water gives you a unique and rather a magical feeling, and the sun makes you feel happy, alive, and full of energy.

This is the power of color!

Here are the main 7 colors and what they embody and stand for:

Red: red can be connected to if you ever want to feel more *grounded*, more connected to the earth. This is helpful when it comes to exams, homework, and if you are feeling too 'floaty,' always daydreaming or possessing great imaginative skills but have been steering away from chores, homework, or responsibilities! It can help with any association of having your 'head in the clouds.'

Orange: warmth! Orange can be used if you have had a fall out with a friend or are particularly upset or emotional about something and generally need to feel a greater sense of love, warmth, and protection. This color may help if suffering from any problems with friends, family, peers, or teachers as it will help heal any emotional wounds and feelings. It is also a great color to help in creativity and artistic expression.

Yellow: Yellow can be connected with to help with confidence, self- assertiveness, and empowerment. It can aid in making good decisions, provide healthy ambition, and sense of goals, and increase your self- worth and abilities. It is also 'sunny', great for speaking, writing, and communication!

Green: Green is a beautiful color for family, friendships (and new love). It increases feelings of warmth, kindness, care, and compassion and relates strongly to nature and the natural world. Particularly effective color to connect to if you feel sensitive or unhappy in any relationship (friends, family). It also relates to love in a universal sense and can increase activities relating to helping the environment or animals and develop empathy.

Blue: Just like the sky and the sea, blue can make you feel calm, at peace, and generally happy. This is because not all of life is sheer excitement, untamed giggles, and bouncing. Happiness is a balance. Blue can help you learn how to feel comfortable 'doing nothing' (or when you have a hard task to do). It calms the emotions and can make one feel at peace with life, your environment, and current situation. It is also extremely beneficial for writing, speaking, and communication!

Purple/ Violet: Dare to dream? Purple and violet are great colors for dreaming, exploring the imagination, and increasing awareness in general. Those 'outside the box' and creative genius ideas arise from the 'energy' associated with the color purple. These colors can be used to aid in memory call, help with learning, and also exploring new ideas, beliefs, and perspectives.

Gold and White: It may not mean much to you now but one day it might.... Gold and white relate to something known as 'the Crown chakra.' This is, in essence, where the spirit comes from. These colors can be used to 'tune into' new ideas, trails of thought and philosophical ideas into our nature. They can be used to explore our cosmic origins and place in society and world at large. All spiritual and 'unseen' phenomena are linked to these colors.

We are essentially rainbows! Use this color guide to help in your meditations.

Chapter Six: Sounds

Exercise: Say, Om

Say, Om! *Om* is the universal sound of creation. It is the sound where, according to many cultures, all other sounds originate.

When we hear the sound our *consciousness*, our conscious mind picks up on it. We receive the *energy and vibrations* that the sound brings. When we speak it, or hum or sing it, not only do we hear the sound with their effect but we also *feel* them. The sound of saying Om rings through our body, changing our *frequency* on a cellular level.

I know what you may be thinking, lots of big words, right? It really is very simple!

Everything in our physical world is made up of vibrations. Just as we enjoy listening to our favorite songs or feel sorrow or emotional from others, the whole universe exists in a state of harmony (or is supposed to!). It is the *frequencies* which construct the physical form of objects, people and things and the *vibrations* which are constantly interacting, shaping the world as we know it.

So saying, singing or humming *Om* can really help with our meditation and our mindfulness.

Sit down and get comfortable. Make sure you are somewhere quiet where you won't be distracted, and start practicing your Oms. Have fun with it and explore all the different feelings and vibrations that come up.

Fun Fact!

Did you know scientists have found that sound waves vibrating at high speeds can make things levitate? *Sound can actually move objects!*

Exercise: Listen to the Birds

When we listen to birds our minds are free to wander. Life turns into a blissful and carefree daydream and all worries and concerns seem to drift away.

This is because bird songs are *healing*, they possess a simple yet extraordinary power. One of the most powerful ways to get in touch with our inner nature and *expand mindfulness*, the ability to be aware of our thoughts and feelings, is to simply be in nature. Animals, plants, and natural life don't have the stresses and concerns we have in our busy and hectic society. There is *a divine simplicity* in the natural world which we can learn from.

Next time you are in nature, stop and listen to the birds. Imagine what they are saying to each other. See them as an intelligent and flourishing community.

Animal Guide: 'Freyja the Nature Fairy!'

Exercise: Mindfulness Mantras

Mantras are words or phrases repeated for greater effect. They can be practiced as meditation or to produce any desired result. For example, 'I will succeed, I will succeed, I will succeed.'

Situations where mantras can be used:-

- To help one study and achieve great results.

- To increase learning, concentration, and focus.

- To aid in mental and cognitive abilities.

- To increase memory, recall, and learning.

- To aid sleep and reduce anxiety or nervous tension.

- To increase feelings of warmth and friendship.

- To overcome fear, anxiety or depression/ feelings of sadness.

- To calm an overactive mind.

- To help bring peace and inner harmony.

- To aid in creative and artistic expression.

- To help imagination.

- To develop relationships with the family.

- To overcome any obstacles and find solutions to problems.

- To increase confidence, self-worth, and feelings of success.

- To help with any desired effect!

As you can see, the list is endless. Mantras are real life 'power-ups' for any element of your life you wish to improve. The key, however, is to speak or think them with *conviction*, with a strong sense of knowing and belief. They can be spoken out loud, whispered, thought during meditation, or even sung.

Next, to each of the points, write a mantra you could use to help you be more mindful and create success. Remember to enjoy yourself!

Animal Guides: 'Eli the Energy Elephant,' 'Freyja the Nature Fairy' and 'Solar the Fire Serpent!'

Exercise: Say Thank You

Saying thank you is one of the most powerful ways to *bring awareness* into one's life. The act of appreciation, to appreciate, increases positivity energy in the thing you are appreciating. So if you are saying thank you to a special person or to a situation or experience bringing you great joy or abundance, you are attracting more of that experience.

You are also amplifying it and enhancing the positive qualities you are appreciative for. Just as light flows into the dark and the rain falls to grow the tree, *life involves a giving and receiving flow*. When we say thank you, and mean it, we are giving positive energy and attracting more of it in our future.

It also helps us be a better person, enhancing beautiful qualities such as humility (to be humble), kindness, and humanness.

Say thank you to everything in your life you are
grateful for and watch the world transform.

Chapter Seven: Movement

Exercise: Conscious Cleaning

That's right kids, cleaning is a conscious activity too!

It is not just your parents you are helping when you do your chores. Cleaning is clearing, it helps free you from any unhappy or unhealthy emotions you are holding onto. It can also help you relax and be calm inside if you have any particularly strong emotions, anger or fears, as the act of *cleaning* can be used to visualize sweeping away your problems. You literally can *sweep away* your worries and concerns.

Did you know there are actually places all over the world people go to clean for free? Buddhist temples and monastery stay in Asia have a mindful meditation clean where grown adults consciously sign up to clean for this specific purpose. They are aware that cleaning and doing chores can lead to *growth and positive outcomes.*

Transform your chores into a 'letting go of the old' act and creating more positivity in your life through this simple yet powerful exercise. Next time you have chores to do, or even better if you wish to help your parents on your own accord, see the whole process as a *refresh*, as a celebration.

With every swipe, brush, and polish imagine all the things you wish to get rid of, all the unhappy thoughts, worries, concerns, and negative emotions. Literally, watch them be cleaned and disappear from your life.

Don't forget to call on 'Melody the Water Whale!' She relates to the waters and can help you see things on a deeper level, providing you a fresh new outlook in life.

Animal Guides: 'Melody the Water Whale,' 'Gracie the Garden Elf!'

Exercise: Movement Meditation

This is another detailed meditation which calls for inner stillness. The only requirements are that you are in a place you will not be disturbed, that you have physical space to move around and that you have access to music. This exercise can be done with friends, peers or family, or alone.

In essence, you can treat this 'Movement Meditation' as a blank canvas, so feel free to combine any of the other practices with this (for example 'Become the Moon,' 'Breathe like a Dolphin,' 'Mindfulness Mantras').

Once in your space, start with breathing. Next, correct your posture and do some stretches. This will loosen up your chi. It is as simple as setting your intention (an important point) like in 'Imagine you are an Owl' so your *awareness* is granted space to be filled up.

At this point allow yourself to move as you wish. Music can be peaceful and blissful, happy, and upbeat or melancholy and reflective. The key is that you *express yourself* in a way that is reflective, mindful, and awake.

Feel free to call on any of your animal guides for help and assistance!

Animal Guides: 'Eli the Energy Elephant,' 'Freyja the Nature Fairy,' 'Solar the Fire Serpent,' 'Melody the Water Whale!'

Exercise: Chi Dance!

Doing a chi dance is one of the most *fun* things to do to increase mindfulness and awareness. It is pretty self-explanatory; when we move, we are allowing our bodies freedom and *our chi is free to flow*. Emotions and stored energy are loosened and we feel *lighter*, also affecting our mind and mental health.

There are many different ways to do a chi dance for mindfulness and your focus can be on anything you choose, anything you wish to embody (like in the 'Play with your Chi!' exercise where you could fill up your ball of energy with any quality you wished). You can also choose to express 'nothing,' no particular thought, emotion or theme and just see where your movement takes you. Now that's really going with the flow!

For the desired effect, however, I would suggest

having a *specific intention* for your chi dance. Call upon Solar the Fire Serpent to help you express yourself, connect to your body and provide your mind with space to wander.

Chi dance!

Animal Guide: 'Solar the Fire Serpent!'

Exercise: Mindful Walk

Walking mindfully is an easy yet effective meditation for greater focus on difficult tasks, clarity, concentration, and inner peace and calmness. It can ease tension or nervousness, help with exams, improve your learning abilities, and increase creativity.

Nature is one of our greatest healers! It is in nature where we feel most at ease, comforted, and happy. Mindful meditation walks are best performed in nature, however, they can be done inside.

To take your meditation to the next level, introduce and combine the following into your walking meditation:

Visualization (visualizing a quality, topic of characteristic whilst walking. Can be combined with other elements)

Imagery (focusing on a specific image, thought or idea in one's mind)

Conscious Breathing (synchronizing your breath to your walking, and any other elements combined)

Observation (choosing a specific animal, item, or color to be mindful of increased observation and perceptive skills)

You will find it is really fun to try, and practice does make perfect.

Handy tip: try combining *Om* and/or *mantras* into your walking meditation!

Also, remember to be careful and if required adults are required to supervise.

Chapter Eight: Creative Expression

Exercise: Learn an Instrument

Learning an instrument, and mastering it is one of the most powerful ways to develop *long-term mindfulness*. Not only does it provide you with the gift of focus, precision, and skill, it also increases *your sense of awareness* and connection to your own self, to others and to the universe as a whole.

Learning an instrument can increase perception, develop concentration, lead to enhanced mental and cognitive abilities, and spark new creative genius!

Call on your animal guides to assist you in making the right choice. If music is your true path you may find you end up playing a range of instruments further down the line.

<u>Handy tip</u>: each animal guide has a *specific energy* and *unique quality*. Which elements resonate with you most? *Water, earth, fire, air,*

ether?

Exercise: Study with Sounds

When we study, our brains require *space, focus, and increased mental abilities* to perform our tasks to the highest standard. The best way therefore to study is *with sound.*

The sound has been scientifically proven to have some rather un*believable* effects. As shared earlier, sound waves (acoustic vibrations) have actually levitated objects, and we all know how happy and good we feel in natural spaces with birds singing or when our favorite songs play.

There are certain sounds that increase one's ability to study, focus, and get through any work with calmness and also a sense of enjoyment. *Studying can be really fun* if you are in the right mind space!

Listen to bird sounds, gentle round sounds, whales or dolphins, or other nature sounds during studying. You can also play wind chimes, Use Tibetan singing bowls and bells and peaceful mindfulness and meditation music for the same effect.

Truly, try it and see for yourself!

Animal Guide: 'Freyja the Nature Fairy!'

Exercise: Write a Poem

Poetry is a great way to *increase focus* and can also be extremely *healing*. To heal is to let go and release, whether that be powerful emotions that are bringing you down, concerns or worries. In addition to the calmness poetry brings to oneself, poems can also act as symbols to our feelings, beliefs, and impressions. Sometimes it really is just better to let things out!

What do you like to write about? What interests you? Nature, animals, and wildlife?

Write a poem for your grandma, aunty, mother or sister (or any of the men in your family). Create something unique to them. Or write a poem for an animal, special plant or spot in nature, something that means something to you. Explore your emotions and feelings towards the object of your poem and then recite it to increase confidence and those amazing lyrical abilities you possess.

You could also write a poem about a monk, or as if you are a monk and explore your thoughts and beliefs about kindness, compassion and peace and what it means to be Buddhist. As Buddhism is all about *mindfulness,* a poem embodying a Buddhist monk could be very beneficial -and fun!

Animal Guides: 'Gracie the Garden Elf,' 'Eli the Energy Elephant!'

Exercise: Drum like a Shaman!

Drumming is a *very powerful* activity for mindfulness. Even when you have let go and are in sheer bliss, it is still a form of meditation.

Ask your parents for a drum, a mini bongo or conga drum will suffice, and explore the various feelings and thoughts that arise. Learn to *synchronize* your breath to the drums and eventually combine visualization techniques with your drumming meditation.

You can use the drum beat and rhythm as *breathing* for all other exercises. There is no power quite like the drum beat!

Fun Fact!

Shamans use drumming to enter a trance state to communicate with spirit! Drumming is a *spiritual experience* for them.

Chapter Nine: Nature

Exercise: Smile at the Sun

The sun is our life force. It gives us vitality, energy, and strength. Without the sun, life itself would not grow and food would not be created for our benefit. We need the sun for *focus, clarity, and concentration.* We also need the sun for *joy, fun, and excitement.* In many cultures around the world, people believe that the sun is a term called '*yang*,' a specific 'force' which allows us to flourish. The opposite is '*yin*'- the moon.

So, if we smile at the sun we are actively giving positive energy, thought, and awareness to this incredible big life-sustaining fire giant in the sky. We receive what we give, so we are also receiving the positive energy and life force from the sun.

Try this short solar meditation for mindfulness.

When you next have the chance, sit down like the monks do, facing the sun. Make sure you are somewhere safe, such as in your own garden or with family if out and about. The key to this is to do it when you are not rushed for time and are outside facing the sun.

With your *focus and attention* solely with the sun, close your eyes and still your mind. Think about all the things that make you happy and are positively associated with when the sun is out. Now, connect those feelings to all the ways they affect you, in a good way. Are there particular fruits or foods you love to eat when the sun is out, friends and company you enjoy or activities that bring you great pleasure? Your list will be unique to you so make sure you really *connect* with those things and *say thank you.*

Appreciation is very powerful!

Keep that list and remind yourself whenever you are down or needing some inspiration of how smiling at the sun made you feel.

The sun will smile back at you!

Animal Guides: 'Solar the Fire Serpent,' 'Gracie the Garden Elf!'

Fun Fact!

Did you know some people live for a certain time on the water, chi, and *sun gazing* alone? *They get their energy solely from nature!*

Exercise: Hug a Tree!

I know what comes to mind. 'I'm not a hippy?'

There is nothing 'hippy' about tree hugging! Without the big, strong-rooted trees we wouldn't be alive, we would simply stop breathing. All living things need love and affection, not just animals and humans. There is actually a science behind tree hugging.

Our thoughts affect our outer world. We can actively influence the wellbeing of others. I am aware a tree is not your mother or animal friend of yours, but trees are *conscious*, they are affected by the sun, rain, and air just as we are. Just as your feline or dog friend needs your love and affection, so does nature. Flowers, plants, crops, and trees all respond to our attitude towards them.

Use any of the mindfulness exercises explored so far to give some love to the trees! *Fill them with chi, visualize them with golden light, or simply think positive thoughts towards them.*

This exercise will not only assist nature but will strengthen your character and mind power tenfold!

Animal Guides: 'Gracie the Garden Elf,' 'Eli the Energy Elephant,' and 'Freyja the Nature Fairy!'

Exercise: Save a Snail

Save a snail! It is very easy to step over one or even (accidentally) stand on one, but *being mindful* of snails on pathways is a great activity to increase awareness and other beautiful qualities. Saving snails is rewarding in itself and can increase feelings of empathy, kindness and care, and compassion.

This is an ongoing meditative exercise and is very good for *developing perpetual awareness*. It can help integrate all other exercises and learnings, allowing them to merge naturally with daily life.

Next time you happen to see a snail in the way or somewhere you know s/he could get stood on, take the time to move it. Not only will this increase mindfulness but it will increase perception, your level of 'sharpness' and attention to detail. Subconsciously (those parts of your mind we don't tend to see but are very real and hidden) saving snails will have a positive impact on the way you respond to people, situations, and animals in the future.

Handy tip: ask '*Freyja the Nature Fairy'* or '*Gracie the Garden Elf*' for their help and protection so other people will pick up on your thoughts and intentions. Remember - *we are all one!*

Exercise: Try a Tea?

Have you ever tried herbal tea?

Chamomile tea is a special flower which brings *calmness and inner peace.* It can help *ease stress* and any anxiousness, also helping with sleep.

Chamomile tea can be drunk to *aid concentration and inner calm before lessons and exams, to deal with tricky or unfortunate situations, and to quiet the mind.*

Drinking chamomile tea, preferably with some honey, is really *good for the nerves* and generally in any situation you need to feel calmer about. Due to the *neurological nature* of the mind and body, chamomile *is great for the mind and mindfulness* and will help in any meditation exercise.

It also tastes amazing!

You can grow it at home (very simple and easy to do) and start a little project. You will enjoy watching them grow and, when ready, the chamomile buds (the heads of the flower) are sweet, delicious, and florally to taste.

They also are loved by bees!

Connect with '***Gracie the Garden Elf***' or '***Freyja the Nature Fairy***' for help with growing chamomile buds.

Chapter Ten: Home

Exercise: Crystal Conscious

Crystals are magical little gems, literally! They are formed over millions of years originating from simple atoms.

Just as there are different colors and frequencies in the electromagnetic spectrum, crystals hold a specific *vibration*. They have been formed directly in the earth, absorbing the energy from our stars, the planets, the sun, and the moon. They have been created from many *unseen and invisible* forces which have a powerful effect on the essence of the gemstone.

Quartz crystals are used to power watches! We can connect to crystals for many great effects.

Use the food meditation for mindfulness exercises to connect to the qualities of the following crystals. Hold one in your hand, close your eyes, and connect to the stillness of the special crystal. You should start to feel a swirling force circling round in your hands.

This is the power of chi!

Quartz: can be used for the imagination, for creativity, and to generally increase learning, knowledge, and wisdom. Can also be used to help induce the feeling of calmness.

Rose Quartz: for the heart! This one can be connected to help with any emotional problems and to increase feelings of love, warmth, empathy, kindness, and compassion.

Amethyst: the 'dream gem.' Purchase an amethyst if you would like to dream more or be open to new ways of thinking. This crystal is great for the mind and deep thinking.

Or use any crystal gifted to you!

Animal Guides: All!

Exercise: Mindful Eating

Let's get straight to it!

Food Meditation for Awareness

Best food types: a rainbow of vegetables, a selection of nuts and seeds, fruits, or your favorite food!

First, you need to choose which food type you wish to *be mindful* with. It's best to stick to one as the purpose of this activity is to explore the different elements of food so you can really connect with it. Nuts and seeds, for example, have a huge variety, from pumpkin, sunflower, and sesame to hemp, chi and flax (just seeds!)

Now, find a calm spot somewhere, somewhere you feel comfortable or by a window with lovely nature views, and close your eye. Hold an item of food in your hand. Don't eat it. At this point, you should naturally feel your belly start to get excited and you will be feeling joy from the feeling of eating that food. But instead, transcend (move past) those feelings. Don't just focus on the potential taste and your taste buds, but change your thoughts and feelings to the food by being at peace with it, connecting with it on an invisible level.

Now, imagine what it smells like. Visualize what the insides look like, the textures, the colors, the potential patterns or unique things that make this divine little gem. Think about how it came to be here in your hands, its journey and all the time, love and work put in by the sun, air, earth, and rain. Say thank you to it, out loud or in your mind. Just focus on your appreciation and love for this piece of food without the desire to consume it.

Once you feel relaxed and calm, smell it. Take in all the scents, possible flavors and feelings you get from the thought of tasting it (but in a controlled way). Meditate. Think and relax your mind on what it will do to your body, on the nutrition and sense of happiness and comfort it will provide. Finally, once you feel completely at one with this piece of fruit or nut or seed or sweet, eat it.

You should feel the difference, yes? The key is that *mindful eating* is an extremely extra-sensory experience and can teach you a lot about yourself.

Call on '***Melody the Water Whale***' if you want a more harmonious connection with food and '***Solar the Fire Serpent***' to help increase your natural chi.

Exercise: Give Someone a Hug!

The divine simplicity of giving someone a hug:

Hugging can be very, very therapeutic. Just through a hug alone sheer waves of happiness can swim through us and make us feel warm, loved, and connected. Of course, we can also help someone feel like this if they were once down!

Hugging releases endorphins, the hormones that make one feel good. So many positive feelings can be created from the simple act of a hug from joy, love, happiness, warmth, comfort, care, compassion, contentment, and bliss!

A scientific study found that we need 12 hugs a day to keep us sustained and nurtured. I don't know how true this is and if 12 specifically is what we 'need,' but it definitely shows how powerful hugs are.

Make a mindful effort to give more things to those you love or friends and family in need. As you are hugging them, *visualize* a pure golden light swirling around them and filling their hearts with happiness. Really *feel* it.

This exercise is powerful for expanding your *visualization* abilities which can help greatly in other activities which call for advanced visualization. Ask for the assistance of any of your animal friends for their power.

Here is a reminder of their unique energy.

Eli the Energy Elephant helps with compassion, feelings of love and warmth.

Freyja the Nature Fairy brings magical feelings through the power of chi!

Solar the Fire Serpent aids in that fiery, excitement to be alive feeling. Helps chi flow.

Gracie the Garden Elf brings comfort and a feeling of home in addition to reminding of your connection to everyone and the natural world.

Melody the Water Whale helps heal and clear emotions and see things from a fresh perspective. In with the new!

Exercise: Be Love

You know by now how powerful your thoughts and intentions are, so what better way to *master mindfulness* than by practicing love and compassion on a daily basis?

Make a conscious effort to remain in a state of mindfulness, even through the hard times. Send loving and positive thoughts out and try to practice compassion and empathy for all living beings.

Remember, your animal friends are *always* by your side.

Conclusion

'Mindful Kids, 40 fun and beautiful activities to increase awareness, focus, and calm oneself,' aims to provide you with direct insight and practical, down to earth, and achievable goals and activities for your journey to mindfulness.

Your animal guides and helpers, 'Eli the Energy Elephant,' 'Freyja the Nature Fairy,' 'Solar the Fire Serpent,' 'Gracie the Garden Elf' and 'Melody the Water Whale' are by your side, even when you don't know it. Once you *set your intention* and commit your mind to mastery they will be there as your 'unseen force,' helping you every step of the way.

Be mindful, be successful!

45680880R00052

Made in the USA
Middletown, DE
19 May 2019